The Basic Essentials of
CLIMBING ICE

by John McMullen

Illustrations by
John McMullen

ICS BOOKS, Inc.
Merrillville, Indiana

THE BASIC ESSENTIALS OF CLIMBING ICE

DEDICATION

This book is dedicated to Mugs Stump. Mugs' achievements were inspirational to me and his adventurous spirit will be missed by all.

Thanks also to Jeff, Greg and Mike Lowe for giving me my first job as an illustrator.

Also, thanks to all the folks at *Climbing* Magazine who keep us all informed of the latest developments in world climbing.

IMPORTANT: The publisher wishes to express the importance of seeking professional instruction from a certified mountain guide before attempting this sport. Ice climbing is an inherently dangerous sport which requires both mental and physical training. This book will prepare you for courses in mountain climbing; it is not intended to act as a substitute for professional instruction.

Published by:
ICS Books, Inc
1370 E. 86th Place
Merrillville, IN 46410
800/541-7323

recycled paper

Library of Congress Cataloging-in-Publication Data

McMullen, John, 1958-
    The basic essentials of climbing ice / by John McMullen ;
  illustrations by John McMullen.
      p. cm. --(The Basic essentials series)
    Includes bibliographical references (p.) and index.
    ISBN 0-934802-87-4 : $5.99
    1. Snow and ice climbing. I. Title.
GV200.3.M36 1992
796.5--dc20
                                     92-21054
                                       CIP

TABLE OF CONTENTS

INTRODUCTION

Climb ice? A bizarre concept I agree, never the less it is an integral part of the mountaineering game. In its purest form, ice climbing is a game in itself that can be played in areas other than mountains. In fact, wherever ice can be found, it can usually be climbed.

I hope the information presented in this book will inspire those of you who have interest in the sport. This book will explain the purpose of ice tools, technique and the attitude needed to become an ice climber.

If you don't have any technical climbing experience, it is helpful to have some basic instruction in rock climbing and be familiar with the equipment involved, most of which is also used to climb ice. There are professional guide services that offer courses in beginning rock climbing.

If you do decide to try it, be prepared. Climbing ice is not a sport for the meek. While you may be freezing out there keep in mind that enlightenment doesn't come to those who do not suffer.

For those of you who already have some knowledge about climbing ice, this book is loaded with information that will add to your own personal experience. No tall tales or photo layouts of famous climbers, just the basic essentials. The illustrations, give clear accurate visuals of equipment and technique, and the text is filled with descriptions of modern methods for climbing ice.

The sport of ice climbing is about curiosity, adventure, technical skill, strength, endurance, perseverance and daring. These are not feelings or accomplishments won while sitting at home reading about other peoples' experiences. Climbing adventures are a chance for the accumulation of valuable knowledge and experience. They are great opportunities to meet and learn from outgoing people, achieve exciting accomplishments, stay physically fit and learn how to deal with fear. All factors that will enable you to be the best you can be. Have fun, and be careful out there!

1. TECHNICAL ICE CLIMBING IN MOUNTAINEERING

Climbing snow and ice has always been a part of the mountaineering experience, mountains at higher elevations typically having glaciers or permanent snow fields. These must often be crossed or climbed during ascent. Knowledge of snow and ice conditions, and how to climb and descend both, are necessary for all climbers traveling in the mountains.

Figure 1-1 Climbing snow and ice has always been a part of the mountaineering game.

1

Traditionally, though not as often now a day's, the first ascent of a peak is made via the easiest route to the top. For many climbers, the first ascent of a peak is not the end of the adventure but the beginning of those to come.

Climbers, in their constant search for adventure, have developed techniques and equipment that help to make the ascent of these routes faster and safer. The time involved in an ascent, is an objective danger that is greatly reduced by the use of modern technique. Changing conditions and falling rock or ice, are hazards that can often be avoided by a fast and efficient climber.

The Equipment Revolution

The later 1960's saw several new developments in ice equipment. The first basic improvements launched a staggering leap in the difficulty of climbing that could be achieved. Climbers aided by the use of a pair of short ice axes with curved picks, rigid crampons and more aggressive technique, attacked the classic alpine routes succeeding with faster and safer ascents. Many climbers, after learning new technique in Europe, went home to search out ice in their homelands. Those in the United States, found many attractive opportunities in the Sierras, the Rocky mountains and in New England. A handful of inventive climbers took this opportunity to develop a few new ideas of their own. Americans like Yvon Chouinard, Jeff Lowe and Greg Lowe have become synonymous with the development of modern ice climbing equipment.

At the same time, an ice revolution was happening in Scotland, Canada and many other countries, all finding that outstanding climbing existed at home. Each added their own improvements to the expanding technology.

The Revolution in the 1990's

There seems to be a resurgence of ice climbing in Europe. The small but numerous ice falls, once overlooked due to summit oriented attitude of European and visiting climbers, are now being climbed with new vigor. Many of the new routes are very difficult and are certain to push modern standards higher.

The competitive attitude of the Europeans has brought on a new twist, the ice climbing competition. Wow! What will they think of next?

Modern Ice Gear

The ice axe, once used primarily as a walking stick, has evolved into a very high-tech climbing tool. This important piece of gear has seen many refinements. The modern ice axe is available in many lengths, with different pick shapes to choose from. Modular construction available on many of the new axe designs, allows the climber to choose the best pick for the type of ice to be climbed. Replace it if damaged while climbing.

Figure 1-2 Modern ice climbing gear.

Ice protection, formerly a skeptical statement, has been improved greatly. The introduction of tubular ice screws has added some security to the sport. This design reduces the fracturing of ice by displacing it into the tube and is quick and easy to place, qualities desired by the ice climber. Ice pickets made of light weight aluminum are useful to both ice climbers and mountaineers. The modern crampon, made for climbing ice and snow is light and easy to get on and off. Most are made with modular construction allowing worn or broken parts to be replaced easily.

Plastic boots are becoming the favorite of the new generation of ice climbers. They are light, have flexible uppers, rigid soles and are very warm.

New technology in fabrics has made active outdoor clothing warmer, waterproof and breathable. Giving the climber more comfort and resistance to the weather.

The Impact of Technology

Great gear will not get you up a climb, but it helps. Technological advances are often controversial, and those in climbing are no exception. If you don't want to use the technology, don't. Those climbers who do embrace the improvements will enjoy the benefits that they bring to the sport.

Today, peaks are being climbed in record time and often soloed by climbers. Many train on the short but severe waterfall routes. The world's best climbers are now taking this experience to new limits.

In 1991, Italian climber Tomo Cesen made the first ascent, solo, of the south face of Lhotse. This bold ascent of an 8516 meter peak in the Nepal Himalaya, will stand as one of the great achievements of modern alpinism.

Jeff Lowe, one of Americas best ice climbers, made an impressive solo ascent of a new route on the north face of Switzerland's Eiger. This face was once the most feared in the world. His new route on this 13,026 foot peak is sixty pitches long and involves grade 6 mixed climbing and 5.10 A5 rock climbing. He climbed it alone! Such climbing was only imagined ten years ago and is testimony to improvements in equipment, technique and attitude of modern alpinist's.

2. ICE CONDITIONS

The ability to identify and determine the quality of ice, is as important to the ice climber as knowing how to use an ice axe. The essential character of ice is caused by the manner in which it is formed, its age and the surrounding air temperature. Its quality will depend on the conditions during this formation and the conditions of the area that the ice has been formed in.

Snow Ice

Snow forms ice known as snow neve and snow ice. As the ice ages it can become blue, green or black ice. Snow neve, snow ice and blue or green ice offer very good ice climbing conditions.

Black ice is very difficult to climb because it is so hard. So hard in fact, that it is difficult to penetrate, which makes it a condition undesirable by many climbers. Snow can cause other conditions that the ice climber must be aware of.

Sandwich ice for example is created by layers of ice and snow. It can be climbed but offers only fair conditions for protection.

Rotten ice is formed when granular spherical crystals bond. Avoid this type of ice as it offers poor climbing conditions and is difficult to protect.

Hollow ice is just what it sounds like, ice that has formed hollow spaces under its surface. This is often caused by melting. This is more common in blue or green ice. Many ice falls have sections of hollow ice. With experience you can learn ways to make use of these formations.

Water Ice

Water ice is usually formed by the freezing and thawing of water rather than an accumulation of melting snow. Water ice climbs are most commonly formed by frozen waterfalls. This type of ice, formed in more seasonal conditions, is more susceptible to change daily. This makes it less predictable than other types of ice.

When it is new and or below freezing, water ice is often brittle and will shatter easily. This makes it difficult to climb and place protection into. The development of the tube ice pick and tubular ice screw has made it a little easier to climb brittle ice.

As Water ice ages it becomes blue or green ice. This stage offers the best conditions for ice climbing, especially if the temperature is just above freezing.

Figure 2-1 Climbing verglas takes a delicate touch.

Be aware of the fact that all of the above conditions can coexist. What is a pure ice climb one day may be an ice and snow climb the next or vice versa.

Other Types of Ice

Verglas is a common condition found on many climbs. This thin coating of ice over rock makes climbing very difficult. Verglas is found more often on less than vertical rock, and caused by freezing water or fog. Climbing verglas takes an especially delicate touch and is difficult to protect because it is so thin.

Rime ice is another condition you may encounter. When water freezes onto a surface that is exposed to wind it will form ice that grows windward. In the right conditions these formations are often solid enough to climb.

Temperature Effects on Ice

The obvious effects of temperature on ice are that the hotter it is the softer the ice, the colder it is the harder the ice. In extremely cold temperatures, ice becomes hard and brittle. And while this is not undesirable it is not a preferred condition. Warm temperatures will give you slushy ice. Slush does not hold ice protection very well, and is wet.

The best temperature for climbing is just slightly above freezing. Temperatures in this range will give the ice a corky or sticky texture that will hold the picks of your ice tools well and provide safer protection. Expect to find the perfect condition of the ice to be inconsistent. You should practice climbing in all conditions (preferably with a top rope) until you learn to deal with all types of ice. Do this before you attempt to lead a difficult ice route.

When planning to go ice climbing the important things to take into consideration are temperature and the position of the climb relative to the sun. The temperature of the ice will change according to the amount of sunlight that directly hits the ice.

Climbs that do not get direct sunlight are often brittle and difficult to protect. If the climb is in the sun however it may be slush by the time you get ready to climb. Plan accordingly.

Falling Rock and Avalanches

The same freeing and thawing process that creates an ice climb also can cause the sport's greatest objective hazard, falling ice or rock. To avoid being hit by falling debris belay from a protected position and

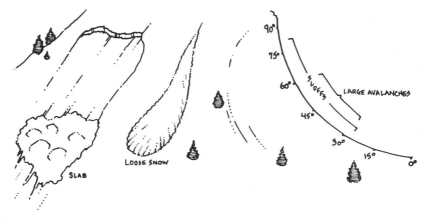

Figure 2-2 A slab avalanche.

always wear a helmet. Also avoid climbing on days when temperature is high.

Avalanche potential should be considered as a serious danger to the ice climber. The gullies in which ice falls form can be highly susceptible to avalanches. Investigate the condition of the area above the climb. If there is any indication of avalanche potential use caution. Negative conditions are heavy snow fall, wet snow or high temperatures and wind-blown snow. For more information on avalanche safety consult *The Basic Essentials of Avalanche Safety* by Buck Tilton (ICS Books, Inc, $5.99).

3. ICE CLIMBING EQUIPMENT

Ice climbing, being a tool dependent sport, necessitates the use of extremely durable, well made gear. Unfortunately, this makes the cost of gear very expensive. Make your decisions carefully and the gear you choose will last longer and give you more enjoyment.

How to Get Started

If you buy your gear in a logical sequence you can build a solid system and not go broke while doing it. After getting outfitted with the right clothing you will be ready to start choosing your climbing equipment.

A good way to get started is to buy your boots first. Try on models made by different manufacturers, all use different last shapes that will give some variety to fit to choose from.

They should fit snug with a sock liner and one pair of medium weight socks. Don't buy them too big, or you will have little control while climbing.

Next, try to put the different models of crampons on the boots. Get a pair that you can put-on and take-off easily. Choose the type that best suits the style of climbing you intend to do.

Choosing an ice axe is a little tougher. It's hard to tell what will work best if you can't try it first. If you haven't used an axe before, you might want to take a lesson from a good guide service to get a feel for the different tools available. Ask them to let you use a variety of tools throughout the lesson. The most important thing to look for is proper weight and balance. How the axe feels in your hand and how heavy it feels while swinging over your head are very important. If it feels good, it will work. If you need two, it is best to get the same brand. Using different lengths is up to you. Buy a good climbing helmet and harness and you are half way there.

If you are interested in buying your own gear I have put together a list of equipment you will need. This includes warm and waterproof clothing needed most of the time while climbing ice.

Clothing list

Silk or synthetic underwear and or fleece tops and bottoms
Medium to heavy, wool or wool blend socks with synthetic liners
Waterproof jacket, pants and gloves or mitten shells
Glove liners made of wool, or synthetic material
Gaiters or overboots
A hat or headband

Climbing gear list

One climbing helmet
A pair of mountaineering boots
One climbing harness
Two ice axes, average length fifty centimeters
One ice hammer (optional)*
One locking carabiner and belay device
One pair of crampons
A small selection of ice protection. Ice screws or pitons*
A small selection of rock protection, Camming units, nuts and rock pitons*
Six to twelve nylon webbing slings and twelve to thirty carabiners*
A 150 to 165 foot eleven millimeter "dry" rope or two nine millimeter "dry" ropes of the same length*
One medium size backpack with two axe attachments and crampon patch
*Some of the responsibility for having this gear can be shared by you and a partner.

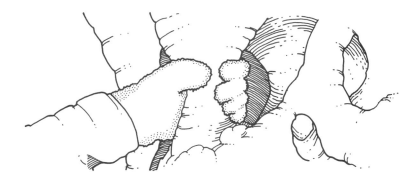

Figure 3-1 Using wool gloves allows you to climb certain features of an ice climb without using an ice axe.

Many people who rock climb eventually try ice climbing, and have much of this gear already. If you're into outdoor sports already, you probably have some gear such as waterproof clothing that will work while climbing ice. If you want to try the sport but don't know how serious you'll get, try a qualified guide service that gives instruction in climbing ice. They usually supply all the gear you will need.

Clothing

Ice climbing is obviously a winter sport, and warm clothing is your first defense against the cold. Traditionally, clothes made of wool were preferred by ice climbers. Wool is warm, and is a good insulator even when wet. One of the most interesting properties of wool is that it will stick to ice. It can be used to assist you when you need to climb in chimneys or sections of a climb where tools are useless or unnecessary.

High Tech Fabrics

Today there are many fabrics to choose from when looking for outdoor sport clothing. Underwear made of synthetic materials such as polypropyline, Capiline™ or Thermax™ is preferred because of their ability to wick moisture away from your skin, keeping you dry. Polarplus™ fabrics used in sweaters and pants are about as warm as wool and weigh less. Outer garments pants, gaiters and jackets can be made of fabrics that are waterproof yet breathable and therefore more comfortable.

Choose products that are well made and designed for use in extreme conditions. Remember, it really gets cold out there on the ice so be prepared. Use a layering system and you'll be ready for any weather condition.

Gloves and Boots

The parts of your body that need the most protection are your hands and feet. Your hands must be able to perform work, such as placing protection and setting up belays or belaying. A light weight glove inside of a heavier mitten or glove will work. Use little elastic loops on the outer gloves so that you can pull them off quickly, even

Figure 3-2 "Idiot loops."

in precarious positions, and not lose them. You will want to do the same thing to your inner gloves if you intend to climb mixed rock and ice routes where you need to climb without gloves. I often use a vapor barrier liner next to my skin. A simple light weight painters glove works well, and only cost a buck at your local hardware store. I don't use a barrier on mixed routes where I have to climb rock. If conditions are wet it's a good idea to carry an extra pair of gloves or mittens. Carry them inside your jacket so they will be warm and easy to get to.

The comfort of your feet will depend largely on the quality of your boots, and whether or not your boots have inner boots or liners. The choice of leather or plastic boots is purely personal. I really like the flexibility and feel of leather boots and prefer them when climbing on warm days when the temperature is not a factor. If you are looking for warmth and light weight, you can't beat plastic. All plastic boots are constructed much the same. The outer shell of the boot is made of durable plastic and all have an inner, boot like liner that fits into the shell. Some manufacturers offer several models of inner boot designed for different temperature ratings.

The type of climbing you do will dictate the type of boot you need to purchase. If you intend to climb mixed rock and ice routes

Figure 3-3 A modern plastic mountaineering boot.

you might want to check out a boot with a rubber band around the base of the shell. This will make it easier to smear into cracks or use on the rock. If you will be climbing in extremely cold conditions you will want a boot with a really warm liner and perhaps even an overboot. An overboot is like a gaiter but covers the entire boot and creates another warming layer. Whatever boot you choose get a good fit. Plastic boots do not really have to be broken in, so the fit you have when you buy them is the fit you will be stuck with. On the other hand if you want to buy or sell a pair of used plastic boots this might work to your favor.

The Ice Axe

Length

Ice axes come in many sizes and shapes. The traditional mountaineering axe, which is sixty to seventy five centimeters long, is an essential part of every mountaineers equipment.

Climbers who want to climb steep ice will want an axe that is forty five to fifty five centimeters long. The shorter size is lighter and allows you to get into smaller places. You want an axe that is light enough to give you the right amount of control, yet long enough to give you good reach.

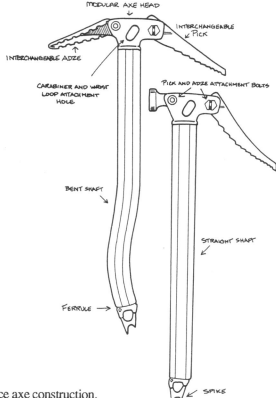

Figure 3-4 Modern ice axe construction.

The Shaft

The strength of most modern ice axe shafts is relatively consistent throughout the industry. All are well made, and most are designed much the same, with the exception of the new Black Diamond axe that has an hourglass shaped shape shaft for a more anatomical grip.

It is nice to have an axe with a good grip. An example would be the coating Black Diamond Equipment puts on their X-15 ice axe. This heavily coated shaft is easy to grip and durable enough to take years of use on snow and ice. Black Diamonds new modular ice axe system, the Black Profit, is made from a specially shaped stock that is coated by the same material used on their X-15 axe. The shape of the shaft adds to the already excellent grip.

An ice axe shaft can be straight or curved. The curved being preferred by climbers who do mostly vertical climbing. The curve of the shaft takes some of the strain off of the wrist while you're hanging.

A straight shaft is my preference for less than vertical ice.

The Pick

The traditional ice axe pick was straight and at a shallow angle to the shaft of the axe. This type of pick works well enough for moderate

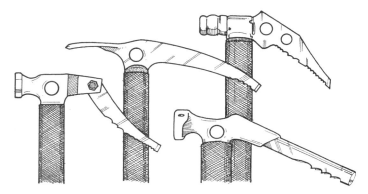

Figure 3-5 Ice pick configurations.

snow climbing but not as well on steep snow or ice.

The modern alpine pick is curved to give the climber better placement with a more natural swing of the axe. This pick works best in alpine ice, but is good for all types of climbing.

The drooped pick is designed for use on vertical ice. It takes a more specialized swing to place this type of pick into solid ice and works best if flicked a few times to create a hole and then hooked.

The reverse curve pick is a variation of the droop pick. By putting a reverse curve on top of the pick, it is easier to remove from the ice. This type of pick is excellent for hooking. The reverse curve pick is preferred by most waterfall climbers.

A very specialized pick design is the tube pick. After seeing how well his tubular ice screw worked, Greg Lowe designed a tubular axe pick made specifically for climbing brittle water ice. This type of pick works best for delicate climbing on brittle ice. Because of the tubular design this type of pick can be very susceptible to damage if hit against rock. It is not recommended for use on mixed or alpine climbs.

Picks for Mixed Climbing

If you intend to do mixed routes where you might have to hook your picks on rock or torque them into cracks in rock, choose a pick that is thin but not so thin that it may crack or bend. Always choose a steel pick for this kind of climbing.

Ice Axe Care and Sharpening

All axes require sharpening. Picks are dulled by regular use and hitting rock in or under the ice. Use a fine hand file to sharpen your axe

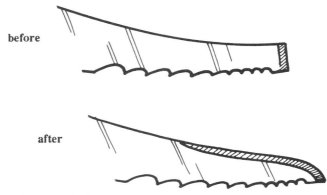

Figure 3-6 Ice pick modifications.

picks. File them to razor sharpness and then dull the edge so it will not bend on itself. If you are using a mechanical or motorized grinder to sharpen tools take care not to damage the temper of the metal. If you find that the pick of your axe is not penetrating the ice very well or that it is difficult to remove you may want to experiment with some modifications to the pick. Better penetration can be achieved by rounding the top of the point of a pick. The teeth on some picks are too sharp or deep. These can be filed down to make removal easier. These modifications are very personal and are easier to experiment with if your axe has modular parts. Modular parts are usually stamped out of steel and unfinished. These parts can become rusted if they are not taken care of. Applying a small amount of oil to all surfaces will take care of rust.

If the bolts used to attach modular parts to your axe are old or loosening while you climb, you can use a product called "Lock Tight" to keep them tight. Apply this before you go climbing. Always inspect your axe before climbing with it. Remove all modular parts and look closely for stress fractures or bent parts. Check slings and wrist loops for damage, wear or loose knots.

Crampons

Two of most important pieces of gear you will use while

climbing ice are your crampons. It's possible to climb sections of ice without using an ice axe, but futile to attempt to climb on steep snow or ice without crampons. Being attached to your boots, crampons are in contact with the ice at all times. There are two types of crampons hinged and rigid that are of interest to the ice climber.

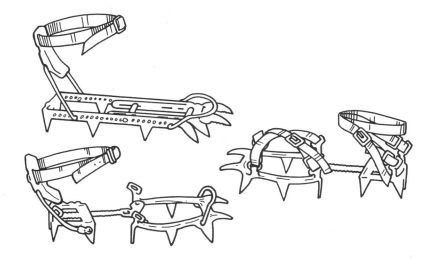

Figure 3-7 Crampons

The hinged crampon is made with two plates connected by an adjustment bar. In use with a semi-rigid boot, the hinged crampon is more comfortable for walking on moderate snow and ice. Since most climbers now use the rigid soled plastic boots many of the newest crampon designs are hinged, this type taking less material to make and therefore being lighter.

Rigid crampons are designed to reduce vibration and give a stable platform on which to stand while climbing very steep ice. The introduction of the rigid crampon was one of the great revolutions in ice climbing equipment and is still the crampon preferred by many water ice climbers.

Crampon Front Points

There are several front point configurations available on crampons. Double horizontal front points are the traditional style used for steep snow and ice climbing. Different manufacturers offer this type of crampon in a variety of point lengths.

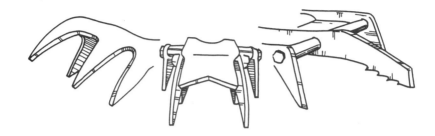

Figure 3-8 Crampon front point configuration

Double vertical front points are shaped like two miniature ice axe picks. They work very well on vertical water ice.

Mono point crampons have one point that protrudes far out of the front and is backed up by two points that are shorter.

The effect is a tripod arrangement which is good for a variety of conditions and works especially well for mixed climbing.

Crampon Fitting and Care

Fitting crampons to your boots is relatively simple. Most are easily adjustable in length and width, and tools for adjustments are usually included with them.

Some crampons need to be sharpened when you buy them. Using a fine metal file, sharpen all points being careful not to take too much metal off. Dull them slightly after sharpening to prevent bending of the points. Always file in the direction of the original cast.

Before climbing always check your crampons for any cracks in the metal, especially the front points. Check modular parts to be sure they are tightened.

Ice Protection

This is what you use to protect yourself on sections of a climb where you might fall. Some of the types of protection made specifically for use in climbing ice are ice screws, ice pitons and ice hooks. The most common being the ice screw. Ice screws are made by many different manufacturers and are available in different lengths. Carrying a mixture of screw-in-screw-out, and

Figure 3-9 A complete selection of ice and rock climbing protection should be combined on your rack.

drive-in-screw-out types on your rack is advisable. They come in short and long lengths but always get the long ones, you can tie them off if they are too long. Short screws are for those of you who are concerned about weight.

The length of a climb will dictate the number of ice screws you need to carry. Don't forget to take enough for the belay.

Rock protection is usually carried and used while climbing ice. A small selection of wired nuts, camming units and rock pitons is all you will need. Take at least six quick draws and a few extra carabiners on your rack.

For more information on ice screws and ice protection see Ice Anchors in chapter 5.

Climbing Helmet

Falling rock and ice are objective hazards of climbing. They are more common in alpine environments. I advise getting a good climbing helmet that is UIAA approved.

Climbing Harness

For ice climbing I recommend getting a harness that is made for alpine climbing. This type of harness has leg loops that can be taken off or undone without having to untie your rope from the harness. This will make it much easier to get your pants down when necessary.

Figure 3-10 An alpine climbing harness.

Ropes

Ropes come in a variety of diameters and lengths. For climbing ice I recommend getting a large diameter rope, at least eleven millimeters thick. If you know how to use double rope belay technique, you might want to use two nine millimeter ropes.

Get a "dry" rope. By this I mean a rope that has a water repellent coating on it. This will help keep it from absorbing too much water that could cause the rope to freeze up or get very heavy.

Backpack

It's important to have a pack to carry all of your ice gear in. I prefer a simple top loading pack with comfortable shoulder straps, padded back, two axe attachment loops and a crampon patch. It should be able to hold at least 2000 to 3000 cubic inches. If you plan on skiing in to a climb you might want to get a larger pack with ski pockets on the sides. The extra internal area will be needed for ski related gear and the external ski pockets are handy for storage of skis while hiking or climbing.

If you plan to put your crampons or axes into your pack, you should get some type of point guards for them. When I put crampons inside my pack I wrap a piece of closed cell foam around them.

Buying Used Equipment

If you can't afford new gear you might be able to find someone selling their used equipment. Take care if you plan to do this though, gear gets roughed up and abused very quickly. Buy modular tools if you can find them, you will be able to replace worn picks or other parts. Always look used equipment over carefully. Check for cracks or loose rivets. If the tools have tape on them beware! Ask the seller if they can remove any tape so that you can check the integrity of the tool. Some of the more modern ice tools are made of very light weight metals. They can damage easily if used by a novice so look at them closely. Never buy a used rope!

4. BASIC ICE CLIMBING

Basic Techniques for Walking on Snow and Ice

While this book is primarily about climbing ice, it is necessary to discuss a few methods used to travel on snow and lesser degrees of ice. This will enable you to climb in all of the conditions you may encounter.

Just walking around the base of an ice climb can be disastrous if you don't know these techniques. Not to mention the fact that you may need to use them on a snowy traverse or descent.

Self Arrest

The self arrest is a method of stopping or arresting from a fall using an ice axe. It's important to practice self arrest technique until you can do it from any falling position, even with your eyes closed! You can learn more about self arrest techniques in any instructional mountaineering book.

While learning to self arrest is necessary, it will do you little good while on ice. The only things that will stop you from falling on ice are, experience, carefully placed protection or a top rope.

The Approach

While walking on the approach to a climb one axe can be carried like a walking stick. Point the pick forward while walking sections that are not steep. If there is a possibility that you may fall point the pick to the rear. This will allow you to get into a self arrest position faster.

Take special care when packing ice gear into your backpack. Cover all exposed points of equipment so they won't puncture your pack or your body in the event of a fall. Lining your pack with a piece of closed cell foam will work nicely.

Skis or snowshoes may be necessary on some approaches. Be sure that you know how to use them.

Walking on Ice

It is important to find a safe area to practice basic technique. Start by finding a flat section of ice at the base of a frozen waterfall, or in a large glacier.

When you find a good practice area, it's best to learn to walk on ice first. Find a safe spot to put on your crampons. Check the straps well, you don't want them coming off! Stand slowly, and gently stomp your feet to get the points of the crampons to bite into the ice.

Remember, you have twelve metal spikes on the bottom of your boots. Don't drag your feet or flail around. A properly sharpened pair of crampons can be dangerous, and you don't want to shred your pant legs.

You will have to lift and place each step. Lift and place your right foot, lift and place your left. Keep your ankles relaxed and flexed. By keeping all the points of your crampon in contact with the surface of the ice you will stick to even the steepest slopes. Should the ice get steep, keep all the bottom points of the crampon in contact with the ice. Flex your knees and turn to face out and away from the ice, climbing the slope backward. You will find that by using this flat footed method you can ascend or descend a slope easily. This method of climbing is referred to as French technique. When practicing this technique, you can use one ice axe for balance.

Front Point Technique

Most modern crampons have points protruding out of the front of their frame. Front points, allow you to face the ice and climb in a more natural position. However, front pointing can cause fatigue in the lower leg if used continuously.

To gain a rest while front pointing, turn one foot out and place it flat footed at approximately thirty degrees to the other. On steep ice look for bumps to place your flat foot on.

Figure 4-1 Flat footed, French   **Figure 4-2** Front point, German
          technique   technique

Use of the Ice Axe

Techniques for Moderate Ice

An ice axe can be used in many different positions. Using the pick of the axe is not always necessary. The techniques described here are for easy to less than vertical ice. Learn them and you will save a lot of energy on a long climb.

The length and type of ice axe you use depends on the degree of difficulty and type of ice you are climbing. An axe that is sixty to seventy centimeters long with a straight shaft is preferred to ascend moderately steep ice. Shorter axes are used when climbing steep ice.

Support Position

If you are ascending a moderate slope hold one axe in support position. Secure the axe to your wrist using a sling, hold on to the head and use the spike or shaft as a third leg. Always be sure you have two points of contact with the ice. This position can be used while traversing and descending also.

Brace Position

The brace position is used when climbing or traversing slopes that are thirty five to fifty degrees. The pick end of the axe is held in the hand that is away from the slope. The other hand is low on the shaft near the ferrule of the axe. The spike is used to brace against the ice. This position works well to aid in balance while using a combination of French and front point crampon technique on steep slopes. The lower foot is placed flat, the upper is on front points.

Figure 4-3 a. Support position. b. Brace position. c. Anchor position. d. Dagger position.

Anchor Position

As the slope gets steeper use the anchor position. This technique can be used on slopes angled forty five to sixty degrees. Set the pick of the axe into the ice above you. Place the hand nearest the slope on top of the axe head, the other hand on the shaft near the ferrule. Front points are used to move feet up. This position allows you to be ready should you need to initiate a self arrest.

Dagger Position—Two Axe Technique

In soft ice that is less than vertical, it is possible to use the picks of your axes as daggers. This technique works very well on less than vertical sections of a climb where you don't want to waste energy placing and removing picks. The two positions for this technique are high and low.

The low position is used on moderate slopes. Place your hand on the top of the axe adze and lean into the slope using the pick for support.

For steeper slopes the high dagger position is used. Reach up to the head of the axe from below and wrap your hand over the pick. Place the pick with a stabbing motion.

Hooking Position—Two Axe Technique

This is the technique used to climb ice steeper than sixty five degrees. The picks of both axes are placed high and the front point of crampons are used to secure the feet. A complete description of this technique is discussed in chapter 8.

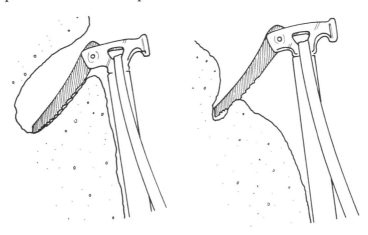

Figure 4-4 Hooking position.

Testing the Condition of the Ice

The first thing to do when you get to the ice is to check its condition. Take an axe out of your pack and test the ice. Set the pick into the ice to see how it feels. Is it soft, or brittle? How secure does the axe feel and how is the ice affected by the pick penetrating its surface? These tests are performed by every ice climber prior to attempting any ice climb. This is the best time to decide if the ice conditions are good or bad.

If the ice is bad, come back another day, or set up a top rope and study the condition of the ice. Take every opportunity to familiarize yourself with the variety of ice conditions.

5. SNOW, ICE, AND ROCK ANCHORS

Ice Axe as Anchor

There are several techniques that can be employed when using an ice axe as an anchor. These are not recommended to be used if a more secure anchor can be set up, but they are useful to know.

Horizontal Axe Anchor

To set this up dig a trench a little longer than your axe and about the same width, horizontally into the slope. Dig another trench about the width of the axe shaft, in the middle of and perpendicular to the first and pointing down the slope.

Using a clove hitch, tie a long sling around the middle of the axe. Place it lengthwise, pick down into the trench with the sling facing the direction of the pull. The axe should be close to the belay side of the trench. Pull the sling tight and clip a carabiner into it. Try not to disturb the snow on the bottom or belay side of the trench.

T-axe Anchor

This is a variation of the horizontal axe anchor with an additional axe involved. Place the other axe vertically in the sling below the axe laying in the trench with the pick facing toward the spike of the axe laying down.

Vertical Axe

Plant the axe straight down into the snow. Tie a clove hitch to the

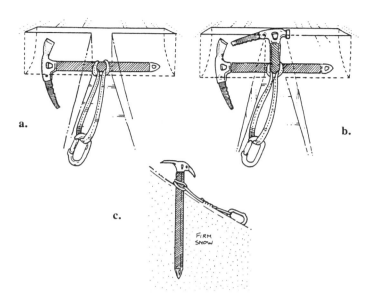

Figure 5-1 a. Horizontal axe anchor. b. T-axe anchor. c. Vertical axe anchor.

axe shaft as close to the snow as possible. Be sure the snow is consistently firm along the entire length of ice axe shaft.

Deadman and Ice Picket

Ice screws are not the only type of protection the ice climber must carry. While most of the climbing is done on hard ice a climber may encounter sections of snow on ledges or at the top of an ice fall. An important piece of protection for such conditions is the deadman

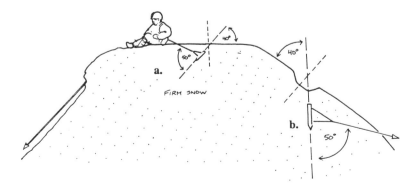

Figure 5-2 a. Deadman placements. b. Ice picket.

anchor. This is a small aluminum plate with a cable extending from its middle. Proper placement takes practice, and snow conditions must be stable enough to hold the deadman firmly in place. Be sure that the snow is not layered.

An ice picket is like a large tent peg. They are commonly made of aluminum to save weight and are used to protect sections of a climb where firm snow has accumulated. The best pickets are made of T-shaped stock aluminum, which gives them holding power and a better strength to weight ratio.

Ice Screws

The most common piece of ice climbing protection is the ice screw. The tubular shape of an ice screw allows it to be placed into the ice with a minimum of ice displacement or shattering of ice. As the screw is placed, ice is displaced into the center of the screw where it is cleaned out after use.

There are many different manufacturers that produce ice screws. The strongest are made of high strength chromolybdenum steel and have ratcheted heads allowing easy removal. Based on experience the two best ice screws you can buy are Black Diamond tube screws, available in two lengths, 22 centimeter and 17 centimeter. And the North American Mountaineering Ice Hog, which is a drive in /screw out tubular ice screw.

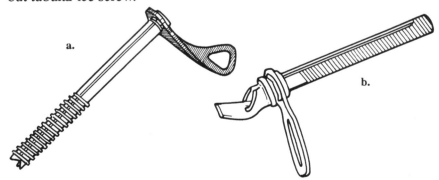

Figure 5-3 a. The Black Diamond ice screw. b. North American Mountaineering's "Ice Hog."

It is important to carry some type of drive in ice screw, as they are faster and easier to place in difficult situations.

Screws made of aluminum and titanium are available but should be used with caution. They tend to break more easily than steel screws and are often difficult to keep sharp. They are also much more expensive. You need not consider using them unless you need to conserve weight.

The Ice Piton

An ice piton is a solid spike that must be driven into the ice surface. This type of protection is more useful in soft ice conditions or in neve ice. Because it is solid and not tubular or hollow, an ice piton will cause serious displacement or fracturing of hard or brittle water ice. It is therefore not recommended for use while climbing frozen waterfalls.

Placement of an Ice Screw or Ice Piton

When looking for a placement there are several things to consider. A piece of protection is only as good as the ice it is placed into. Look for the solid ice to set your protection into.

Consider how your partner will remove it. Avoid placing protection in corners or deep between icicles. Try to place protection from a comfortable stance and within reasonable reach of the stance.

An ice screw should ideally be placed angled slightly upward at ten to fifteen degrees past perpendicular to the surface of the ice. Clear

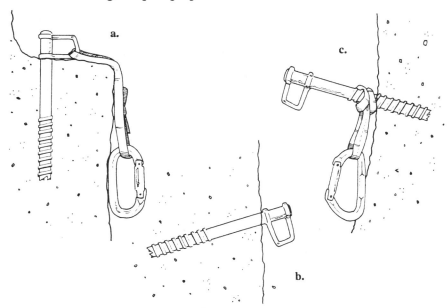

Figure 5-4 The proper placement of an ice screw is a critical factor in the overall strength of the protection. a. Horizontal placement. b. Vertical placement. c. Tie-off.

off any soft layers of ice to reveal the most solid ice, leaving plenty of room for the ratchet or eye of the screw or piton to rotate during placement and extraction. Be sure the ice is solid and deep enough to accept most or all of the length of the screw. If you cannot sink the screw in to the eye, tie it off. Attach a runner to the shaft of the screw by using a clove hitch tied as close to the surface of the ice as possible. This is to reduce leverage on the screw that could cause it to fail under the force of a fall.

Extra Precautions

Use caution while placing a screw. If you feel any change in resistance while hammering or tightening a screw remove it and look for another placement. If you are tightening a screw and you feel an increase in resistance you may have hit rock. Stop immediately, especially if you are using aluminum or titanium screws, as you will damage the teeth. If there is enough of the screw in the ice tie the screw off as close to the ice as possible.

If the climb you are doing is getting direct sunlight cover the exposed portion of ice screws with ice or snow to avoid heating and melting that will weaken the placement.

The Ice Hook

The Black Diamond Spectre is a new twist on an old principle. While the use of hooks is traditional in rock climbing it is a new concept in ice climbing protection.

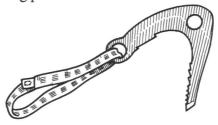

Figure 5-5 Black Diamond "Spectre" ice hook.

Ice climbers are used to looking for hook placements for their ice picks because such placements are more secure due to less fracturing of the ice.

The Spectre can be hooked into holes up to four inches deep. Made of chromolybdenum steel, a Spectre can be driven into ice or even into small cracks in rock.

Using the Ice

Often the formation of an ice fall will offer some natural forms of protection. It is best to be aware of all the possibilities while climbing ice.

One of the most common features of ice is the icicle. A large icicle that is joined at the top and bottom can be tied off with a long sling to offer a good point of protection. Smaller features can be used with caution and should always be backed up by an ice screw or piton if possible.

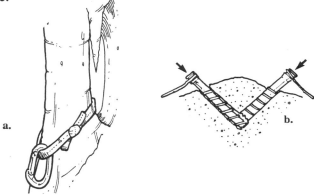

Figure 5-6 a. Tied off icicle. b. Hour glass.

An ice hourglass anchor can be formed by placing two ice screws at a minimum of six inches apart at converging angles to form a channel. A piece of cord is then passed through the channel using a wire hanger as a guide and then tied off with a water knot or grapevine knot. Care must be taken not to fracture the ice between the holes.

A feature most often overlooked, and a good source of protection, is the mote along the edge of an ice fall. Camming devices

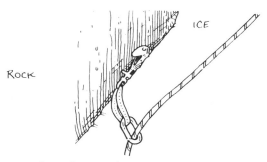

Figure 5-7 Using the mote for rock protection.

can be placed in this crack much the same as in a crack on rock. Lowe Tri-cams work well in this type of placement as do Black Diamond Camalot's.

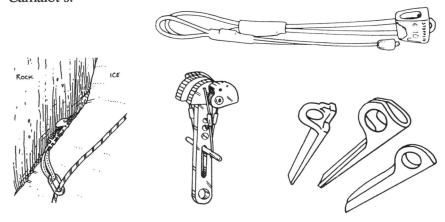

Figure 5-8 Rock protection that may be useful when climbing ice.

Rock Protection

Often, it is possible to find placements for protection in the rock along side an ice fall. A selection of nine wired Stopper Nuts and a set of Camalots will be sufficient for most climbs.

Pitons are not an accepted form of protection on free climbs or most big wall climbs due to the fact that they permanently damage the rock. They are however a commonly used method of protection for ice and alpine climbs. This doesn't mean that you shouldn't try to use clean climbing protection. It is acceptable to use a piton if you cannot find safe placements for clean gear. A selection of six different pitons is common on an alpine or ice climbers rack of gear.

6. BELAYING

One of the most important anchors in ice climbing is the belay anchor. It can also be one of the most confusing to set up, especially if it's a hanging belay. All of the anchors discussed in chapter 5 can be used in a variety of combinations. It will take some time and experience to get to know all of the possible variations and the amount of security they offer.

Setting up a Belay in Ice

This is a sample of a possible scenario you may encounter. The anchors will be ice screws but in a realistic situation you might substitute them with other types of protection.

When you reach the end of the pitch look around for the most stable section of ice. Place a screw to one side of your stance, not in the middle. Clip a carabiner to the screw, pull up some rope and tie off to this with a figure eight knot.

Place another screw a couple of feet away from the first, horizontally. Put a carabiner on the screw, and tie in with a clove hitch. Pull some slack from the clove hitch if necessary, and tie a figure eight in the middle loop of rope.

Using a locking carabiner, clip the figure eight to your harness. Then clip another locking carabiner to the carabiner on the second screw. Tell your partner you are off belay. Pull up the rope from below,

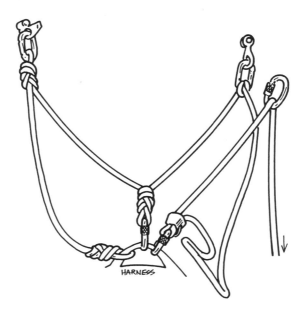

Figure 6-1 Belay set-up on ice.

until it gets tight. Clip it through the second locking carabiner on the screw, and then into your belay device. Your partner is now on belay.

Well, that was easy. Now let's tackle a tougher situation. Setting up a belay on ice can be a test of your creative abilities. Don't get too dialed into doing the same thing all the time. You need to think of new ideas and use them.

Steep Ice—The Hanging Belay

You've reached the end of the pitch, and the end of your rope, but there's no stance. A good position to get into is with one axe placed about a foot and a half above your shoulder, arm slung through the wrist loop. With your other arm get a screw off of your rack. Hold the screw in your high hand and hammer it in with your other hand. Clip in and get in another screw at least a foot away from the first. After independently tying off the screw and clipping into the locking carabiner on your harness, back up the anchors by tying your ice axes into the system.

Have your partner take you off belay. Pull up the rope until taut and clip it into a locking carabiner on one of the ice screws. Using a Munter hitch or a belay device put your partner on belay. Easy, enough

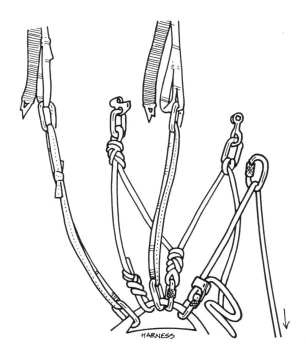

Figure 6-2 Hanging belay on ice.

said! This takes a lot of practice to perfect.

It is best to know all you can about every type of anchor before you try to set up a hanging belay. There are many variations and by being creative a secure belay is usually attainable in any given situation.

Snow and Ice Bollards

Any natural ice feature that a sling or rope can be looped over and around safely is considered a bollard. A well formed bollard can be used as an anchor for belaying or rappelling. An ice bollard is

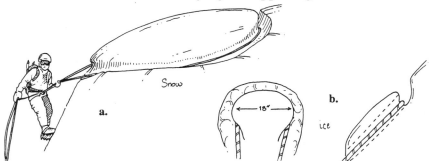

Figure 6-3 a. Snow bollard. b. Ice bollard.

probably the strongest anchor you can use while belaying on ice.

It is possible to create a man made bollard in snow or ice. A snow bollard can be created by stomping your feet to make a channel for the rope. A shovel can be used in soft snow or an ice axe if the snow is very firm. The size of the bollard depends of the constancy of the medium. In soft snow make sure the rope is laying in the channel along the line of the firmest snow. A pick or ice axe can be added to the upper edge to reinforce it during a belay or rappel. When rappelling the reinforcement should be taken out before the last man goes down. You might have to flip a coin for this honor!

A bollard made of ice can be much smaller than one made of snow, and if made carefully is stronger than an ice screw. Ice bollards are generally cut into ice using the adze of an ice axe, although the pick of the axe or an ice screw will work with a little more difficulty. The minimum size of an ice bollard should be no less than twelve inches wide, at least twenty inches long and six inches deep in good ice. A notch in the top will help keep the rope in place.

Special care should be taken when constructing an ice bollard. If there is any indication that the bollard is not sound construct another one.

Although it takes some time to construct a bollard, they are a good option for retreat or rappels allowing you to get down without leaving any gear.

Belay Techniques and Devices

Today most climbers use some type of belay device such as a stitch plate, figure eight or tuber. These are great most of the time but it is a good idea to know how to do a Munter hitch belay. The Munter

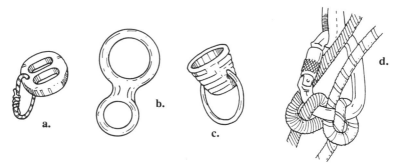

Figure 6-4 Belay devices. a. Stitch plate. b. Figure eight. c. L.A.S. Tuber. d. Munter hitch knot

hitch is a knot, that when used with a large locking carabiner provides a very safe and less mechanical belay than most devices.

Sitting in a Stance

If you are belaying from above you can increase the integrity of the belay by getting into a good position in the snow. Seat yourself as

Figure 6-5 Getting a good stance will add to the security of a belay. a. Standing. b. Sitting.

deep into the snow as possible with your feet spread apart. Keep the line from you to the belay anchor tight.

7. DESCENDING

"It ain't over 'til it's over"
Yogi Berra

After reaching the end of a serious ice climb you might think that the adventure is over, hold onto your hat because the fun is just beginning.

Descent Support Position

When walking down ice you will find that the flat footed French technique can be used. If you need a point of balance for steep sections use one axe. Facing out, keep your knees bent and place the pick of the

Figure 7-1 Descent support position.

axe a full reach below you. As you lift and place each foot flat on the ice use the shaft as a hand rail. In this crouched position, you will have to stomp your crampon points into the ice hard to get them to stick.

When you reach the head of the axe pull it and place it below you again. Continue this technique until you are down.

Descending From an Ice Climb

Unlike many rock climbs, ice falls rarely have fixed anchors at the belay stations. Though luckily, trees or rock boulders are fairly common on shorter routes and can be slung to provide very solid anchors for a descent. Some times you can hike down from the top. On an ice route where these features can't be found the ice climber must be creative in setting up anchors for the descent.

Descent Anchors

In order to save most of your expensive ice protection you need to know how to make anchors that will allow you to descend using no gear, a minimal amount of gear or an inexpensive alternative.

A good anchor to use during a descent is the ice bollard, or snow bollard discussed in chapter 6. This type of anchor is strong and will allow you to descend without leaving any gear. However, bollards are difficult and time consuming to construct, and therefore not many climbers will attempt to make them unless they are gripped.

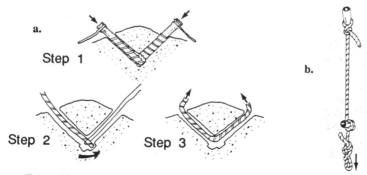

Figure 7-2 a. Hour glass anchor b. Electrical conduit anchor.

Icicles, should be used with caution because they are not as strong or predictable as other types of anchors. Use only a very large one if it is the only anchor available.

A man made ice-hourglass anchor will work very well for a descent anchor but you will have to leave a piece of sling. This type of anchor is very strong.

Another alternative is the use of electrical metallic tubing, or electrical conduit as it is commonly called. This tubular material can be cut in any desired length and be placed in a pilot hole created by an ice screw. The best configuration for this type of anchor is vertical. Two anchors tied together with an overhand slip knot on the top anchor and a clove hitch on the lower using seven millimeter cord. The rappel rope is threaded through a knot in the end of the cord. More detailed information and the results of testing on the ice-hourglass anchor and the Electrical conduit anchors are available in the February/March 1991 issue of Climbing magazine.

Rock gear can also be used to descend from an ice climb. It is less expensive than ice gear and therefore easier to part with. Camming units can be rigged so that they can be removed from below.

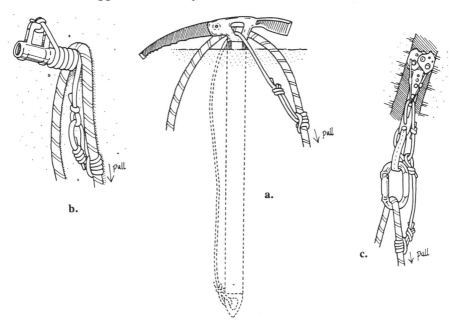

Figure 7-3 Descent anchor retrieval. a. Ice axe. b. Ice screw. c. Camming unit.

Techniques for the Retrieval of Equipment Used on a Descent

The methods illustrated above are used to retrieve three different types of protection. Take special care that you don't get hit by the gear when it falls!

8. CLIMBING VERTICAL AND OVERHANGING ICE

Very steep ice forms with sections of vertical ice topped by ledges or bumps. Even easy ice climbs will have vertical steps that have to be climbed.

Climbing vertical ice takes strength, technique and an aggressive attitude. Your state of mind must be focused and confident. Technique and strength will not take you to the top of each vertical section. You must be self assured that you can conquer them.

This Is It

Since we are discussing the most difficult level of ice climbing here, I want to mention that falling while leading a serious ice route can be extremely hazardous to your health. Climbing safely at this level is a matter of experience, not one of technical knowledge. Discover your own abilities by starting out on routes that you can top-rope. Practice placing protection on those routes that are within your ability.

Attitude on Vertical Ice

Maintaining good balance and body position will make vertical ice less intimidating. The attitude you must have to lead steep ice is one of total control, knowledge of all ice conditions and the technique used to climb them. It's totally up to you to decide when you're ready to take the next step.

Figure 8-1 Maintaining good balance and body position will make vertical ice less intimidating.

If you have any doubt or reservations about leading a particular route you may not be ready. I'll tell you the truth, it's normal to feel a little queasy at the start of a climb. Keep your head, take your time and always be prepared to retreat if you get too gripped.

Leading a Pitch

As you start up the ice, reach out with your tools, placing the picks into the ice at a comfortable height. Don't throw too high. If you're standing on your toes, you're reaching too high. Doing this will cause your front points to shear out of the ice. Keep your crampons at a ninety degree angle to the ice most of the time while you are front pointing. Lowering your heels a little is more comfortable. If your crampons second set of points are angled forward they will bite into the ice in this position.

Figure 8-2 a. The power throw. b. Climbing thin ice.

When the ice is thick and in really good condition, you can use a "power throw" to place the picks. By bringing the axe behind your back and throwing the pick into the ice, you use the larger muscles in your chest and therefore save energy. When using this technique, be careful to concentrate on the spot you want to hit with the pick.

Thin ice takes a very delicate touch. If the ice is thin, tap your pick into it creating a small hole. Gently hook your pick into the hole without jerking on it and pull. When you bring up your feet you can hook a front point into the hole you created with your pick. Mono-point crampons work very well for this technique.

After placing both tools walk your feet up. Don't take big steps. Some climbers will look above them for another axe placement while one foot is higher than the other. If they see a good placement, they pull one axe, reach up and place the tool higher than the other. This technique is aggressive but works really well because you tend to get better rhythm between placements. Don't be afraid to be aggressive! When you're actually out there doing this, you can laugh at how easy it sounded here.

If you choose to place both axes high and walk your feet up evenly be careful that you don't bring your feet up too high. In a scrunched position such as this it is often difficult to get the picks of your axes out of the ice. Move your feet up until your hands are approximately waist high. Then you can raise and lower the shaft until the pick is free or grab near the top of the axe and pull the pick straight out. Never twist the pick by using a sideways motion while you try to remove it. Cold temperatures make metal brittle and twisting could cause the pick to break.

As you climb look for bumps on the ice both for your pick placements and to kick your crampon into. Often you can hook features and lightly kick your crampons onto the tops of bumps. This is especially useful when climbing brittle ice.

If you are not the first to climb the ice fall on the day you are climbing, you may be able to hook much of the climb. Look for the placements of the other climbers and set your picks into the holes. Give them a jerk to test their integrity and cruise!

Climbing ice by hooking, is much easier physically than having to make the holes for your picks. But beware, the head game is still there.

Overhanging ice is rare. It is usually found under a bulge in the rock where the water is pushed away from the rock as it freezes. The formation of the overhanging section is surrounded by icicles that can be broken off and used to stem between as you climb out and over the bulge.

Figure 8-3 Correct rope management will save time and energy. a. Single rope technique. b. Double rope technique.

Figure 8-4 Hooking allows you to save energy for the more difficult sections of a climb.

Resting

On steep ice it is difficult to find a comfortable stance that will allow you to rest. Stemming in a corner or ice chimney is an effective stance that will allow you to balance most or all of your weight over your front points, thus giving you an opportunity to rest your arms. By bending your knees you can lower your heels and take some of the strain off of your calves. Use your axe for balance.

Another position for resting is called the "monkey hang." This is basically a straight-arm-layback hang from your waist loops, with your feet high. To get into position place both ice axes at equal height. Then work your feet up under you. To rest your right leg, bring your left foot up level with your rear and in front of you. Your right leg is placed practically straight out to your right side, flat footed. Rotate your ankle so that all of the crampon points are in contact with the ice. This position is reversed to rest the other leg.

Take advantage of any rest that you can find, but don't hang out too long or you'll get pretty cold. If your hands start to get cold, and

Figure 8-5 Resting stances. a. A stem. b. The monkey hang.

they will since you have them over your head most of the time, you can hang from one tool and lower the other until you get some warmth circulating through the hand.

Placing Protection

You have to look ahead of you to plan a stance for placing protection. Often you can plan where you will place protection from the start of the route or from a belay. If you can't see far enough above you to plan your route, you will have to, as they say, "feel it out."

Placing ice screws is a chore. Placing them on a vertical ice climb is even worse and can often be the crux of an ice climb. If you have ever seen an ice climber with more than two ice screws within a twenty foot section of vertical ice it is a rarity, or he's aid climbing. Due to the difficulty of placing screws on steep climbs many climbers opt for the cruise method. Climb until you are about to wet your pants, then slam in some protection!

It is easiest to place protection from a good stance but these are sometimes difficult to find. If you can place protection while standing

Figure 8-6 Placing protection. a. Straight arm technique. b. Arm slung through wrist loop. c. Hanging from daisy chains.

on a ledge or while in a comfortable stemming position, go for it!

A straight arm hang works well on steep ice. Place your axe high. Hang from the wrist loop with a relaxed grip. If you wish for a little added security you can attach a daisy from the axe to your harness. With your other arm, place your hammer in the ice or in a holster on your harness. With your free hand, take a piece of protection off of your rack and place it using the hammer if you need it.

Another method is to place your axe so that the wrist loop is a little above your shoulder. Loosen the wrist loop and slide your forearm through until the wrist loop is at your elbow. Place your hammer in the ice or in a holster. Take the protection off of your rack and place it.

The last method, which is considered aid by some ice climbers, is to have daisy chains attached to both ice axes. Both axes are placed high and the climber hangs from them while placing protection with a third tool. Now it can be told!

Climbing Icicles

Climbing icicles or freehanging icicles that are not attached at

Figure 8-7 Climbing a freehanging icicle.

the bottom—is a sport in itself. Great care should be taken and you should have extensive ice climbing experience. This style of climbing is extreme, and calls for a special book of its own. Well Alex L., we're waiting!

Aid Climbing

Whenever a tool is used directly, to rest or to ascend a formation of ice it is considered aid. Aid climbing is considered bad style for those on the cutting edge of ice climbing. But, it is used regularly by those of us who are still human. One of the aid techniques used by mortals is the hang and rest. This technique has

Figure 8-8 Resting on points of aid.

many forms. From the basic place a screw—hang—and rest, to a cowstail attached to the harness which is looped over the ice axe pick and hung from. I personally, will do whatever is necessary to get a rest when I need one.

Staying in Control

Moving around on ice is difficult. When you're climbing ice you are surrounded by very sharp objects that can turn you into a pin cushion if you're not careful. Always move precisely and in control of your tools.

Figure 8-9 Tap your axe shaft against the sides of your boots to avoid snow build up on bottoms of crampons.

Use special care when walking over sticky snow with crampons on. Snow can build up on the bottoms of crampons creating a platform that will keep the points from sticking into the ice. This can be disastrous. Use the shaft of your axe to tap the snow off if this is happening.

9. GRADING OF ICE CLIMBS

It's traditional in climbing to grade a climb after its first ascent. This information is offered as a guide to those climbers who wish to repeat the route. Often, the accuracy of the grade depends on the experience of the first ascent party. Grades are usually given for MODERATE or NEUTRAL conditions. If the conditions are different than those during the first ascent the grade will not be accurate.

Giving an ice climb a grade of difficulty is somewhat speculative. It's easier to rely on the grade given an alpine route. Alpine ice is more permanent and less likely to change on a day to day basis. Water ice, on the other hand, is rarely stable for very long and grades are not often a good indication of the condition you may encounter.

The grade of a climb is based on the condition of the first ascent or the historical condition of the ice fall. It should be considered only as a guide to assist you in attempting a climb within your ability.

The traditional grading system used through out the world is the Scottish Grading System. Using Roman numerals I through VII, each numeral describes length and level of difficulty.

Grade I: Short routes on moderately steep snow or ice, the angle of which is usually less than fifty degrees.

Grade II: Longer, slopes of snow or ice. Higher angle sections or steps of rock, snow or ice.

Grade III: Climbs that may have sections nearing vertical. Steep, long ridges with vertical sections.

Grade IV: Difficult climbing. Sustained sections of vertical ice, snow or mixed climbing.

Grade V: Very long and sustained routes. Many difficulties, such as steep vertical ice, snow or mixed climbing.

Grade VI: Very difficult climbing. Routes of a more alpine nature that involve long approaches and extreme commitment.

Grade VII: Long and very difficult routes at high altitude in the Himalaya or other extremely remote mountainous areas.

American climber, Jeff Lowe has added a technical difficulty grade scale to the overall difficulty scale of the Scottish Grading System. This scale, which starts with a designation for the type of ice such as, WI for seasonal water ice and AI for permanently alpine ice and is followed by a numerical scale from one through seven. One indicating a technically easy ice climb and seven indicating an extremely difficult technical ice climb.

Rating a climb using this system would look like this.

The Black Ice Couloir, Grand Teton, Grade IV, AI 3.

This indicates that the amount of time needed to do the route is typically one to two days, the type of ice is permanent alpine ice and the climbing is difficult. Now in reality, the conditions could be easier or much more difficult depending on the season that you climb in, or the amount of snow and ice in the couloir at the time.

Rock Grades

Occasionally there are sections of rock climbing involved on an ice climb. This is referred to as mixed climbing.

Rating these sections requires the use of the local rock climbing grading system. In America the Yosemite Decimal System is used. This system grades the difficulty of rock climbing involved. Grades one through four cover terrain from walking to scrambling over steep rock where a rope is not necessary.

The fifth grade is an indication that a rope and some equipment is needed for safe progress. This grade, indicated by a 5 is broken down into decimal points of 1 through 14 and points 10 through 14 are broken down further into a, b, c and d.

Free Climbing Grade (Yosemite Decimal System)
5.0 - 5.5
5.6
5.7
5.8
5.9
5.10a, b, c, d.
5.11a, b, c, d.
5.12a, b, c, d.
5.13a, b, c, d.
5.14a, b, c. That's as hard as they get for now!

Free climbing is a term used to describe a style of climbing in which the climber ascends the rock using only their physical strength. All equipment used in free climbing is for safety. The free climbing grades seldom get higher than 5.10 when combined with an ice climbing grade.

Aid Climbing Grade (Yosemite System)A1 - A5

Aid climbing signifies the direct use of equipment to ascend sections of rock that cannot be free climbed.

The condition of an ice climb can change from moment to moment. Use the grading system as a guide. Always be prepared for the route to be more difficult than the rating. You may be happily surprised to find the climbing is easier than the grade indicated.

If I'm thinking of doing a specific ice climb, I will ask climbers in the area if they've climbed the route recently and what kind of conditions I can expect. Sometimes this isn't possible, so you have to go look for yourself. More times than I'd like to count, I've gone to a climb only to find it's not in condition to undertake. That's when I slap on the ski's and practice my telemark turns!

©1991 MCMULLEN

APPENDIX A

BIBLIOGRAPHY OF ICE CLIMBING AND RELATED LITERATURE

Barry, John, Snow and Ice Climbing, Cloudcap, Seattle, 1987.

Bearzi, Michael, "Doing The Mixed Thing.", *Climbing*, February 1992, pp. 101-103.

Chouinard, Yvon, Climbing Ice, Sierra Club Books, 1978.

Cordery-Cotter, Robert, "La Glace Extreme.", *Rock & Ice*, January 1991, pp. 78-83.

LaChapelle, Edward R., The ABC of Avalanche Safety, 2nd Ed., The Mountaineers, Seattle 1985.

Long, John, How to Rock Climb, Chockstone Press, Inc., Evergreen 1990.

Lowe, Jeff, The Ice Experience, Contemporary Books, Inc., 1979.

Luebben, Craig, "The Ins and Outs of Ice Screws.", *Rock & Ice*, January 1991, pp. 84.

March, Bill, Modern Snow and Ice Techniques, 2nd Ed., Hunter Publishing Inc., Edison, NJ, 1988.

Peters, Ed, (ed.), Mountaineering—The Freedom of the Hills, 4th Ed., The Mountaineers, Seattle 1982.

Raleigh, Duane, "Chill Out.", *Climbing*, December 1991, pp. 98-99.

Selters, Andy, Glacier Travel and Crevasse Rescue, The Mountaineers, Seattle.

Toft, Murray, "Getting Down on a Shoestring.", Climbing, February
   1991, pp. 100-103.

INSTRUCTIONAL ROCK CLIMBING VIDEOS
Long, John, The Art Of Leading, VHS, color, 50 mins.
Long, John, Basic Rock Climbing, VHS, color 45 mins.

GLOSSARY

Adze: A blade on the head of the ice axe designed for cutting steps or for climbing soft ice.

Aid: When a climber is directly using protection to ascend.

Alpine climbing: Long climbs in the high mountains which involve rock and ice climbing.

Alps: High mountainous areas in Europe are referred to as Alps.

Anchor: Any device or object that secures the climber to the medium being climbed.

Avalanche: A dangerous condition caused by an unstable accumulation of snow. A sliding mass of snow.

Belay: A method of stopping a falling climber using rope.

Belay station: The position of the belay on the climb.

Big wall: Very large rock walls that often take days to climb.

Black Diamond Equipment: The largest manufacturer of climbing hardware in the United States. The only manufacturer of ice climbing equipment in the U.S.A.

Black ice: A very hard and difficult to climb type of ice.

Black Profit: Black Diamond Equipment's modular ice axe.

Blue ice: A ice condition which appears blue in color. This generally indicates good ice for climbing.

Bollard: A snow or ice anchor either natural or man made, that is shaped like a large oval door knob.

Brittle ice: A condition which occurs when temperatures are below freezing (32 degrees). It appears as clear ice.

Camalot tm: The trade mark name of Black Diamond Equipment's camming unit.

Camming unit: A device made with logarithmic cams. These come in many different configurations, some are mechanical, some are not. the design allows the protection to be placed in parallel sided cracks of varying sizes.

Capaline tm: The trade mark name of Patagonia Clothing's synthetic wicking fabric.

Carabiner: A snap link made of aluminum that is an integral part of climbing protection systems.

61

Chromoybdenum: A strong but light metal used in manufacturing of many climbing tools.

Clean climbing: The use of protection devices that do not damage the rock.

Clip-in: Any junction in the protection system where a carabiner is used.

Closed cell foam: Foam made for insulation. Often used for sleeping pads.

Clove hitch: A knot that can be created in any section of a climbing rope. It is very adjustable and is used most often at belay stations to equalize anchors.

Couloir: An ice or snow filled gully.

Cowstail: A large loop of perlon rope.

Crampon: A metal frame with points protruding out of the bottom and front that is attached to the boot of the climber. When used properly they enable boot so stick to the ice.

Dagger: A technique for climbing ice using only the pick of the ice axe.

Daisy chain: A small rope or webbing ladder approximately three feet long. Used to adjust the height of the climber in relation to the protection while aid climbing.

Deadman: A plate of aluminum with a long cable attached to its center. It is used as an anchor in firm snow.

Dry rope: A rope treated with a water repellent substance is referred to as a dry rope.

Electrical conduit: Tubular aluminum material which is cut into sections and used as a replacement for ice screws during descent from a climb.

Eye: The part of a screw or piton where the carabiner is attached.

Ferrule: The ferrule holds the spike to the shaft of the ice axe.

Figure eight device: A rappel device shaped like an eight.

Fixed anchor: A piece of gear that is permanently placed in the rock and left for the safety of other climbers to follow.

Fleece: Synthetic insulating fabric used in clothing.

Free climbing: A method of climbing whereby the climber uses only his or her physical strength to ascend. Equipment is used only for safety in the event of a fall.

French Technique: A flat footed technique used to climb ice.

Front points: The points that extend from the toe of a crampon.

Front point technique: Sometimes referred to as German technique. This is a method of climbing steep ice face using only the front points of the crampons.

Gaiter: Commonly made of waterproof material gaiters are designed to keep snow out of boots.

Gear: Ice or rock climbing equipment.

Grade: A number given to indicate the difficulty of a climb.

Gripped: A common expression used by climbers to indicate fear or high anxiety.

Guide service: Organizations that offer climbing instruction and guided climbing.

Hanging belay: A belay while hanging from protection.

Harness: A webbing seat that distributes the force of a fall to the upper legs and waist of the climber. A harness consists of leg loops for both legs, which are connected to a belt around the waist. The climbing rope is tied directly to the harness.

Head: The top of the ice axe between the pick and adze.

Hollow ice: Ice that has holes below its surface caused by melting.

Holster: A small loop attached to the climbing harnesses waist, used to hold an axe while not in use.

Hook: Metal hooks that are used in pockets or on ledges for protection or direct aid.

Hooking: A technique whereby the pick of an ice axe is hooked into holes in the ice.

Hour glass anchor: An ice anchor created by drilling two holes that converge and then threading a sling through the hole.

Ice Axe: Commonly referred to as an ice tool. The ice axe acts as an extension of the ice climbers arm and hand while climbing ice.

Ice Hog: Made by North American Mountaineering, the Ice Hog is a drive-in-screw-out ice screw with a ratcheted head for easy removal.

Ice Screw: A metal tube with treads and an eye to clip into, used for protection when climbing ice.

Last: The form on which a boot is constructed. This is what gives the boot its shape.

Layback: A climbing technique. A sideways position where the arms are pulling and the feet are pushing as they walk up the surface being climbed.

Layering system: Layering clothing using various insulating fabrics.

Lock Tight: A compound used to keep bolts from loosening.

Locking carabiner: Carabiners with screw or spring loaded sleeves that stop the gate of the carabiner from accidentally opening.

Mixed climbing: A climb that involves ice and rock climbing together.

Modular: Constructed of parts that are interchangeable or replaceable.

Monkey Hang: A method of resting while climbing steep ice.

Mono Point: A crampon with a single point protruding out of the front.

Mote: A small slot along the side of an ice fall caused by melting.

Munter hitch: A knot used for belaying.

Neve: A firm type of alpine snow ice.

Nut: Wedges of aluminum that are placed into cracks in rock and used as protection.

Objective hazards: Situations that are out of the control of the climber such as falling rock and weather.

Overboot: Like a gaiter but made to cover the entire boot. An overboot protects the boot from moisture and the extra layer of material adds some warmth to the boot.

Overhang: Any section of ice or rock that is at an angle of more than ninety degrees.

Pick: The point on the head of an ice axe used to climb ice or for self arrest.

Picket: A large tubular or t-shaped peg used as piece of protection in firm snow

Piton: A metal spike that is hammered into cracks in rock and used for protection.

Point guard: Protective covers for crampons or ice axe.

Polarplus: The trademark of Malden fabrics synthetic fleece material.

Polypropyline: A moisture wicking fabric used in underwear.

Quick draw: Short sewn loops of webbing used between two carabiners. Used on most pieces of protection to allow free movement of the rope and to reduce rope drag.

Power throw: An energy saving method of placing the pick of an ice axe.

Rack: The selection of protection and other equipment taken on a climb. Commonly carried on a sling over the head and shoulder of the lead climber.

Rand: A rubber strip that wraps around the boot above the welt which aids in climbing rock.

Rappel: A rope technique used to descend from a climb.

Ratchet: A device used to remove ice screws. Some ice screws have ratchets incorporated in their design.

Rime ice: An ice form created by wind and moisture.

Rotten ice: Poorly bonded crystals make this type of ice opaque in color.

Route: The line taken by a climber on an ascent or descent.

Sandwich ice: Created by layers of different types of ice.

Self arrest: A method of stopping while falling on snow or soft ice.

Shaft: The part of an ice axe between the head and the ferrule.

Sling: A loop of nylon webbing. Slings are used for many purposes while climbing.

Snowfield: A large area of permanent snow.

Solo: to climb alone, with or without a rope for safety.

Spectre tm: The trade mark for Black Diamond Equipment's ice hook.

Spike: The bottom most point of an ice axe.

Stance: A safe and relaxed position from which the climber places protection, rests or belays.

Stem: A spread eagle position where all or most of the climbers weight is placed on the feet pushing outward.

Stitch plate: A simple belay device.

Stopper tm: The trademarked name of Black Diamond Equipment's aluminum wedge nuts.

Stress fracture: A crack in metal caused by fatigue or a blow against rock.

Temper: The hardening of metal by heat.

Thermax cm: A synthetic fabric from Dupont used in sports clothing. Thermax is a light weight hollow core fiber that wicks moisture away from the skin and offers excellent insulation from the cold.

Tie-in: The point where the rope is tied to the harness or wherever a knot is used.

Tie-off: A small loop of webbing tied to a piece of protection. Its position close to the surface of the ice or rock reduces leverage on the piece of protection.

Titanium: A light weight metal used to reduce the weight of equipment.

Top rope: A method of belaying a climb where the anchors are placed at the top of the climb prior to an ascent. The belay rope runs from the climber to the top and back down to the belayer. When properly set up, top roping is a very safe system to use when learning to climb.

Torque: When the pick of an ice axe is placed in a crack and rotated while climbing on rock. A mixed climbing technique.

Traverse: Any sideways movement while climbing or descending.

Tri-cam tm: The trademarked name of Lowe Alpine Systems non mechanical camming device which can be used in rock or iced cracks for protection.

Tuber tm: The trademarked name of Lowe Alpine Systems belay/rappel device.

UIAA: The Union Internationale des Associations d'Alpinisme. This group, represented by individuals from all participating countries, studies the equipment used for climbing and gives UIAA approval to that equipment which meets their standards for maximum security.

Vapor Barrier: Any waterproof material which creates a barrier keeping heat and moisture close to the climbers body.

Velcro: Or hook and pile as some call it, is a product used on many types of outdoor clothing and accessories. Consisting of two strips of material, one with a fuzzy texture the other with small hooks. When joined they stick together.

Verglas: A thin layer of ice over rock.

Webbing: Made of woven nylon, webbing has many uses in the manufacturing of climbing equipment.

Wool: A natural material used in fabric. A very warm insulator against cold. It will retain heat even when wet.

Wrist loop: A Sewn of tied sling made of webbing which is attached to the head or through a hole in the shaft of an ice axe. Wrist loops enable the climber to hang from his wrists rather than by gripping the shaft.

X-15: The name of Black Diamond Equipment's interchangeable pick ice axe.

INDEX